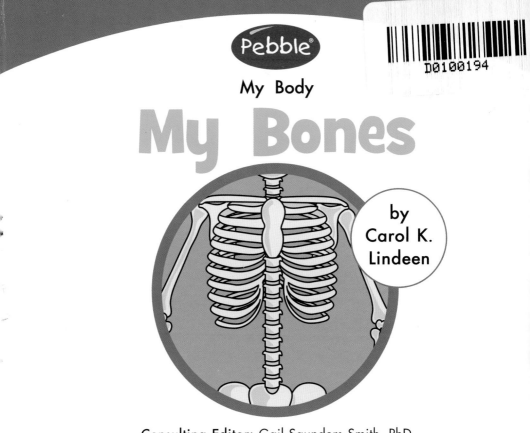

Pebble®

My Body

My Bones

by
Carol K.
Lindeen

Consulting Editor: Gail Saunders-Smith, PhD

Consultant: James R. Hubbard, MD
Fellow in the American Academy of Pediatrics
Iowa Medical Society, West Des Moines, Iowa

Capstone
press®

Mankato, Minnesota

Pebble Books are published by Capstone Press,
151 Good Counsel Drive, P.O. Box 669, Mankato, Minnesota 56002.
www.capstonepress.com

1 2 3 4 5 6 11 12 10 09 08 07

Library of Congress Cataloging-in-Publication Data
Lindeen, Carol, 1976–
    My Bones / by Carol K. Lindeen.
    p. cm.—(Pebble Books. My Body)
    Summary: "Simple text and photographs describe bones and human
skeleton"—Provided by publisher.
    Includes bibliographical references and index.
    ISBN-13: 978-0-7368-6696-5 (hardcover)
    ISBN-10: 0-7368-6696-5 (hardcover)
    ISBN-13: 978-0-7368-7840-1 (softcover pbk.)
    ISBN-10: 0-7368-7840-8 (softcover pbk.)
    1. Bones—Juvenile literature. 2. Human skeleton—Juvenile literature.
I. Title. II. Series.
QM101.L56 2007
611'.71—dc22   2006013828

Note to Parents and Teachers

The My Body set supports national science standards related
to anatomy and the basic structure and function of the human
body. This book describes and illustrates bones. The photographs
support early readers in understanding the text. The repetition
of words and phrases helps early readers learn new words. This
book also introduces early readers to subject-specific vocabulary
words, which are defined in the Glossary section. Early readers
may need assistance to read some words and to use the Table of
Contents, Glossary, Read More, Internet Sites, and Index sections
of the book.

Table of Contents

My Bones 5

On the Inside 13

My Bones and My Body 17

Glossary 22

Read More 23

Internet Sites 23

Index 24

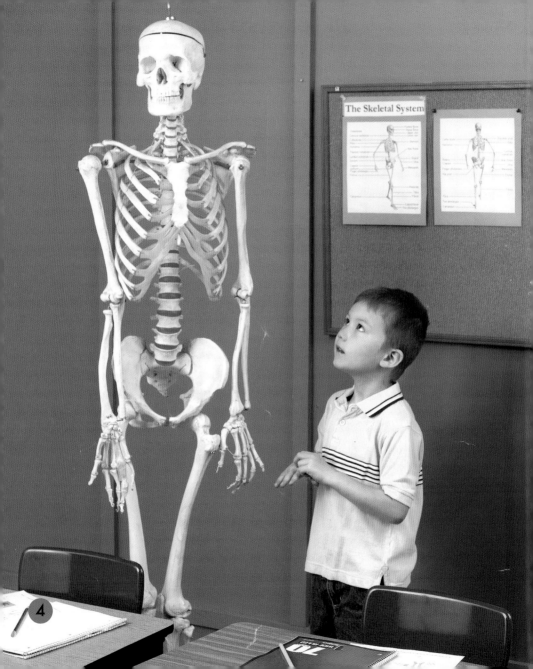

My Bones

My bones help me
stand and move.
I can't see my bones,
but I can feel them
inside me.

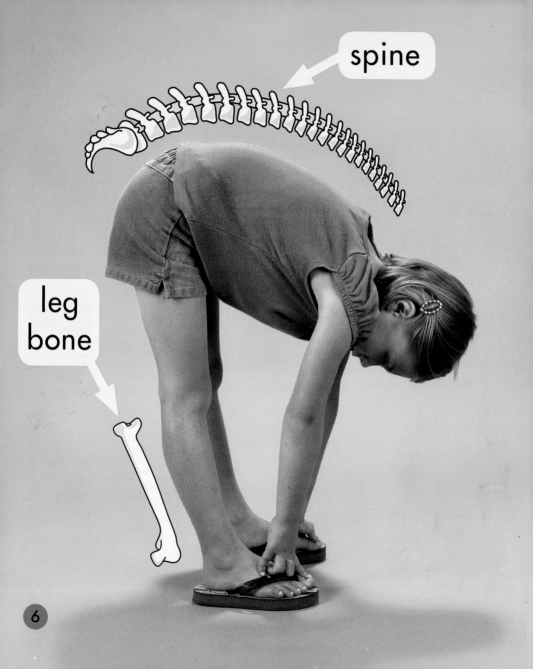

spine

leg
bone

My bones are
many shapes and sizes.
My leg bones are
long and straight.
Small bones in my back
make up my spine.

8

13
FEET DEEP

I can feel my rib bones
in my chest.
My rib bones protect
my heart, lungs,
and stomach.

ear bones

I even have
three tiny bones
inside my ear.
They are the smallest
bones in my whole body!

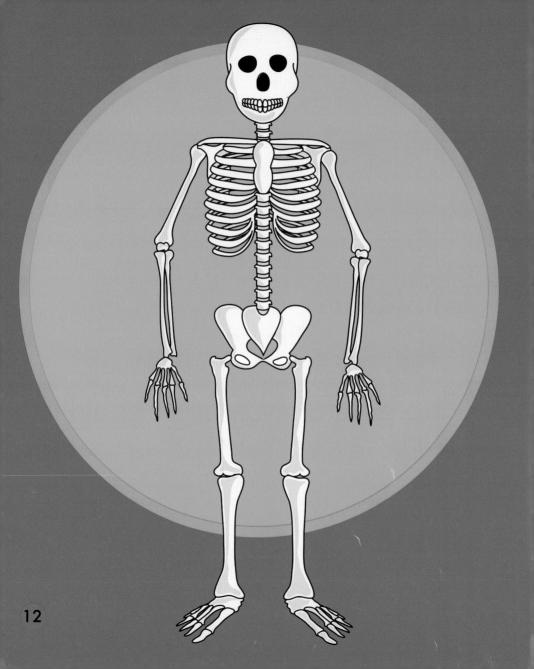

On the Inside

All my bones make
up my skeleton.
My skeleton gives
my body its shape.

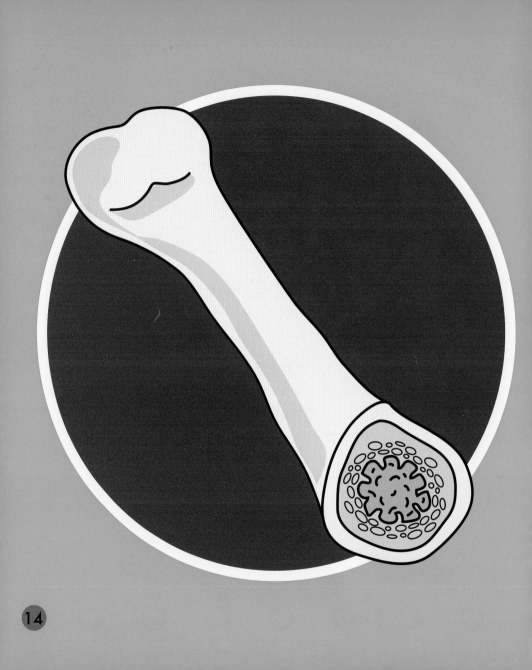

My bones are
hard on the outside
and soft on the inside.

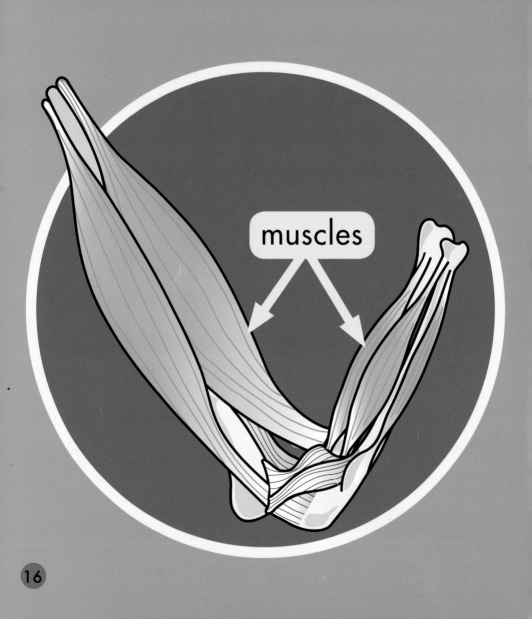

muscles

My Bones and My Body

Muscles connect
to my bones.
My muscles help
my bones move.

A joint is where
two of my bones meet.
My elbow is a joint
that bends back and forth.

EAT **5** A DAY
for better health

I drink milk
and eat good food
to keep my bones
healthy and strong.

Glossary

joint—the place where two bones meet; knees, elbows, hips, and shoulders are joints.

muscle—a part of the body that makes movement; your muscles are attached to your bones.

protect—to keep something safe from harm or injury

ribs—curved bones around your chest; your ribs are connected to your spine.

skeleton—the framework of bones that supports your body

spine—your backbone; your spine is made up of many small bones called vertebrae.

Read More

Gray, Susan H. *The Skeletal System.* The Human Body. Chanhassen, Minn.: Child's World, 2004.

Nettleton, Pam Hill. *Bend and Stretch: Learning about Your Bones and Muscles.* Amazing Body. Minneapolis: Picture Window Books, 2004.

Internet Sites

FactHound offers a safe, fun way to find Internet sites related to this book. All of the sites on FactHound have been researched by our staff.

Here's how:

1. Visit *www.facthound.com*
2. Choose your grade level.
3. Type in this book ID **0736866965** for age-appropriate sites. You may also browse subjects by clicking on letters, or by clicking on pictures and words.
4. Click on the **Fetch It** button.

FactHound will fetch the best sites for you!

Index

bending, 19
chest, 9
ear bones, 11
eating, 21
elbow, 19
healthy, 21
heart, 9

joints, 19
leg bones, 7
lungs, 9
moving, 5, 17
muscles, 17
rib bones, 9
shapes, 7

sizes, 7, 11
skeleton, 13
spine, 7
standing, 5
stomach, 9
strong, 21

Word Count: 148
Grade: 1
Early-Intervention Level: 14

Editorial Credits
Mari Schuh, editor; Bobbi J. Wyss, designer; Sandy D'Antonio, illustrator;
    Wanda Winch, photo researcher; Kelly Garvin, photo stylist

Photo Credits
Capstone Press/Karon Dubke, cover; TJ Thoraldson Digital Photography, 4, 6, 8,
    10, 18, 20